W9-BIZ-209

LITTLE MERRY SUNSHINE
HE'S NOT . . .

. . . but hilarious he certainly is. So smooth
life's little rough spots with the most lovable loser
around—Herman. And look for him in:

**"AND YOU WONDER, HERMAN, WHY
I NEVER WANT TO GO TO ITALIAN
RESTAURANTS!"**

**"APART FROM A LITTLE DAMPNESS,
HERMAN, HOW'S EVERYTHING
ELSE?"**

"WHERE'S THE KIDS, HERMAN?"

**"IN ONE OF YOUR MOODS AGAIN,
HERMAN?"**

All available from Signet

More Big Laughs from SIGNET

HERMAN

"Any Other Complaints, Herman?"

by
JIM UNGER

A SIGNET BOOK

NEW AMERICAN LIBRARY

Copyright © 1979 by Universal Press Syndicate

Published by arrangement with Andrews, McMeel & Parker

The cartoons in *"Any Other Complaints, Herman?"*
appeared originally in *The 1st Treasury of Herman.*

"Herman" is syndicated internationally by
UNIVERSAL PRESS SYNDICATE

SIGNET TRADEMARK REG. U.S. PAT. OFF. AND FOREIGN COUNTRIES
REGISTERED TRADEMARK—MARCA REGISTRADA
HECHO EN CHICAGO, U.S.A.

SIGNET, SIGNET CLASSIC, MENTOR, PLUME, MERIDIAN AND
NAL BOOKS are published by New American Library,
1633 Broadway, New York, New York 10019

First Signet Printing, June, 1985

    3 4 5 6 7 8 9

PRINTED IN THE UNITED STATES OF AMERICA

"The Doctor says he'll see the gentleman with the smallpox first."

"I gotta write a poem about Dad. What rhymes with 'el dummo'?"

"If you don't keep quiet I'm gonna phone all your friends and tell them how old you really are."

"Meadows, the doctor says I need more
exercise, so I want you to start jogging for me."

"I guess I can borrow a magnifying glass to show it to the girls at work."

"Why did your nurse want to know my 'next-of-kin'?"

"The capital of Holland is 'H.'"

"Well, the window's open. I hope you're satisfied."

"If my dad asks you what you do for a living, say
you're a marine biologist!"

"Visiting hours are 2 'til 4 p.m."

"Now you're in Grade 4, Daddy's not going to be able to help you with your homework anymore."

"If you don't go to sleep, you're gonna be
practicing that swing in a wheelchair."

"I'm putting you on probation. That means no more mugging for 12 months."

"So sorry I woke you!"

"Every summer we get another rash of
'Littlefoot' sightings."

"You wouldn't let me have a dog. You wouldn't
let me have a cat!"

MATERNITY

"False alarm. Your wife had an inflamed gall-bladder."

"I haven't changed much since I was 18, have I?"

"He's trying to figure out a way to clone himself so he can stay home all day and still get a paycheck."

"If you'd buy me a dishwasher, you'd have more time to help out around here."

"His bark's a lot worse than his bite."

"When I was your age, I was the only one to have an engagement ring that squirted water."

"You can't blame tv if you're dumb enough to walk up to a 300-lb. truck driver and say, 'Ring around the collar.'"

"How is it I take a shower every day and do it with-
out stepping on the soap?"

"Get this straight! If people only retire when
they're no longer productive, you should've
gone 10 years ago!"

"Good morning, sir. Is your wife home?"

"You say it was silver, cigar-shaped and had the
letters U.F.O. painted on the side?"

"I can't find my clean underwear."

"Did I hear you right? Did you just tell me I'm
starting to put on weight?"

"This one's supposed to go, 'snap,
crackle, BOOM!'"

"Whaddyer mean, it's only a model? How much
bigger d'you wanna build it?"

"D'you realize we've been married three whole weeks and neither of us has even mentioned the word 'divorce.'"

"It'll go away if you don't keep looking at it."

"Listen, there's nothing wrong with being ambitious."

"Grandma, I can see where Dad gets his whiskers!"

"You didn't forget to pay the window-cleaner again?"

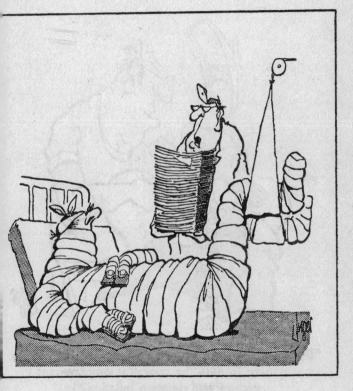

"I've got the results of your X-rays."

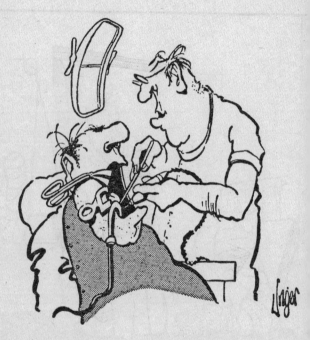

"Do you think the current economic policies will do
anything to ease the overall unemployment
picture and dampen inflation?"

"I had to dig it all by hand."

"Browning, for a guy who's worked here 12 years, you're setting a lousy example."

"I bet your mother's pie wasn't as soft as that."

"Wake up, Daddy."

"It's a piece of wood!"

"Don't laugh, my wife thinks I'm in South
America with two million bucks."

"We can put all our old junk up here."

"This is your last chance. If you scalp this one, you're through."

"Come along, Polly. Let Mr. Herman finish his coffee."

"The results of your tests were negative. Get lost!"

"I'm well aware it's only a plastic sword.
Don't interfere!"

"Your wife phoned. She said if you want toast for breakfast, bring home a loaf of bread!"

"Mr. Henderson, he's written another check!"

"Why don't you go to a proper dentist?"

"They say opposites attract. There must be
plenty of good-looking, intelligent girls around."

"Now, imagine you've cornered a bear and he runs into a disused house."

"Even as a kid I was a slow eater."

"You MUST know how you got in there."

"The Marquis of Halifax writes, 'The vanity of
teaching doth oft tempt man to forget
he is a blockhead'."

"Slice of wedding cake?"

"You're looking a lot better today, Ralph."

"I've changed my mind. I'll have a
cheese sandwich."

"Where did they get him from?"

"Sorry!"

"I've got two other applicants to see before I
make my final choice."

"I know it's sudden—but I want a divorce!"

"If you read the instructions, dummy, you'd see there's one switch for drying and another for styling."

"I think we're in trouble. He doesn't even know
what a car is!"

"Bermuda triangle."

"What are the chances of becoming a pirate?"

"Did you win?"

"She gets nervous when we use the new cups."

"Abdul...will you keep that thing outa sight while we're still in the oil business."

"Your mother's out in the yard."

"You'd better get a good grip on that net, Herman."

"Seeing you once a month is gonna make
the next two years a lot easier."

"Here's the coffee . . . right at the back."

"If you Jane, me Harry."

"While you're taking time off from work, just
remember where you got the germs."

"I sometimes wonder if you hear one word I say!"

"Cold lunch today . . . I'm going out."

"Isn't it time he went to bed?"

"You're not supposed to just pour the stew into
the lunch pail."

"If she has one more birthday, this whole place is gonna go up!"

"Herman, I've never known a guy like you for
hitting them in the water."

"If you've got any screaming to do, wait until you get off the premises."

"I'm glad their Apollo program is over, I was getting sick of taking this net down every five minutes."

"It says; 'Come in number 10, your hour's up!'"

"It's getting so you can't trust anyone anymore."

"If you don't buy one of these pencils, you're
placing an unfair burden on the rest of society."

"Would you believe it? I've been all over town trying to get you some flowers."

ABOUT THE AUTHOR

JIM UNGER was born in London, England. After surviving the blitz bombings of World War II and two years in the British Army, followed by a short career as a London bobby and a driving instructor, he immigrated to Canada in 1968, where he became a newspaper graphic artist and editorial cartoonist. For three years running he won the Ontario Weekly Newspaper Association's "Cartoonist of the Year" award. In 1974 he began drawing HERMAN for Universal Press Syndicate, with instant popularity. HERMAN is now enjoyed by 60 million daily and Sunday newspaper readers all around the world. His cartoon collections, THE HERMAN TREASURIES, became paperback bestsellers.

Jim Unger now lives in Nassau, Bahamas.